MW00652229

A Mother's Nightmare

*My Battle With Breast Implant
Disease And The Opioid Crisis*

Started by Stacy Shain

Finished By Bonnie Shain, Mother

Edited by Dr. Mark Katz, Cousin

TO MY CHILDREN:

CAMERON, SIERRA AND JAX

The highlight of my life was being with you

Always remember how much I loved you

Always remember the good, fun, and happy times we shared.

Our fun games, vacations, and family

Hi-My name is Stacy Ann Shain. If you are reading this now, it means I did not make it. I began jotting down information on this terrible journey and battle with my Breast Implant Disease/The Opioid Crisis and have instructed my mother to complete it upon my death. You see, many people have had this disease and have survived. I would have survived as well if not for my Spinal Tap and three blood patches. The pain in my body was bad, but the head pain was unbearable. I believed something was sent to my brain during the blood patches, after a botched spinal tap, done in the first place to find out what was wrong with me. Nobody listened and nobody took the time to try to figure it out. And because of that, I am no longer here, without my babies, without my mother, my family and my friends.

I am Bonnie Shain. Stacy's surviving devastated mother. Here is our story:

⌒

On September 6, 2019 Stacy's funeral gathered more than 400 people. Her brothers each recited a eulogy, as did her sister-in-law Alli and best friends, Ivy and Erika. I would like to begin Stacy's story with the eulogy from her older brother Jeff:

> "What do you say at a time like this? I know I am supposed to say I feel sad right now, that this is a tragic loss of life and issue some meaningless platitude, but right now, in this moment, all I can feel is anger. Anger at a healthcare system that failed my sister. Angry at doctors too overworked and understaffed to do their job properly. Angry at a prescription system that dispenses pills like candy and profits from that irresponsibility. Anger for losing my sister the night

before my wedding and watching my already frail marriage unravel because of it. Angry that my niece and nephew will spend the rest of their lives without a mother and my parents without a daughter. But mostly, I'm mad at the universe that grants us the gift of existence that comes with a cost everyone must bear, a brief life, and somehow in that brevity we are expected to find meaning and purpose and accept that is enough. Well, I don't accept it. How can you give a person something so wonderful as life only to take it away? This isn't fair, but fairness was never a part of the bargain, was it? Chaos, it seems is the only reliable force in the universe. Stars are born from the nothing, burn bright and bring life and light to all that can stand witness. Then one day, like all things, they die and grow cold. My sister was a star. A radioactive, beautiful, profane, disobedient, talented young woman with an entire life ahead of her. I may never understand what happened to her, and even if I did, it will never fill the hole in my heart. I will miss my sister with the power of a thousand suns. My only consolation staring into the faces of her young ones she left for us to care for. I wish I could offer you all something more, a memory, an anecdote, but I simply cannot summon the will. This is all I feel now.

Sincerely,
Jeffrey A. Shain-Stacy's oldest brother

From Bonnie Shain, Stacy's mother:

On July 19, 1985, having had two sons, my daughter was born. I had been a gymnast, then a girl's gymnastic coach since my teens, and I had always dreamed of having a little girl. To say the least, I was elated beyond words. I said to the doctor, "Let's go out for breakfast and celebrate." He said, "don't move". I could not wait to call my gymnastic team and the whole world and tell them I had a daughter.

When Stacy was only a month old, we were stunned to find out that she was visually not following anything. We took our daughter to Dr. Mulvey, a fantastic ophthalmologist who would follow my little girl until she was 21. She had to tell us to find an adult ophthalmologist; otherwise, we would have continued seeing her. Stacy later took her own children to Dr. Mulvey to make sure their eyes were okay. On that first 1985 visit, she told us that Stacy simply had "delayed vision," that her eyes looked good, and that normal vision would come upon her. However, after Stacy's first DPT vaccination, she developed all three types of nystagmus-oberal, vertical and horizontal. We then took Stacy back to her pediatrician, Dr. Z, who told us that it was likely she probably had deeper neurological problems. I spent the next few days crying. Stacy was then taken to Wills Eye in Pennsylvania and further learned that she had night blindness as well. It traumatized me seeing wires sticking out of her eyes in the dark. I held her hand. It didn't seem to bother her as much as it did me. They talked us into doing a spinal tap to rule out any neurological problems; this all happened when she was only three months old.

I remember that day like it was yesterday. They sent in a resident to retrieve the spinal fluid. He looked at my little girl too nervously (for me) and I said "You get one shot, otherwise go get a doctor". And he did. After the test was done we learned that Dr. Mulvey was right all along. Nothing neurologically was amiss. We changed pediatricians! We stayed with our new ones- Dr. Lopez/Dr. Emanuel until Stacy was 21. (Stacy later on would use Dr. Emanuel for her own three children). One conclusion that came out of the workup-so-far, was that Stacy should not be given the "P" (stands for Pertussis) in the DPT immuni-zation injection ever again. This may have been a decision that saved her eyes because by the time she was ten months old, the nystagmus had disappeared. Unfortunately Stacy's vision was awful. We were told her vision was 20/2000, which is legally blind. (Later on, she would be able to wear special contacts which corrected her vision to 20/60). This was Stacy's first introduction to a foreign substance. We did not know, at the time that she had the MTHFR homozygous gene, and doctors at CHOP are debating whether or not the MTHFR had something to do with the very bad reaction with her eyes, to the DPT vaccination.

When Stacy reached a year old, she had the onset of what sounded like a breathing problem. Her father and I videotaped her sleeping and drove the evidence to her pediatrician, who lived down the block, and who then sent us to an ENT specialist. Stacy's tonsils and adenoids were so enlarged, they were obstructing her breathing and had to be removed.

Entering kindergarten, she had to wear glasses so thick that on her first day, she was bullied and made fun of. I remember the glasses being so large on her little five year old face. That was the first protective incident I had with my little girl. I called those parents and resolved that STAT! Midway through kindergarten Stacy was already putting in her own contacts. My goal was for her, even at that young age, was to become independent and eventually be able to drive. (When she became of driving age, she had to take a course three times until I felt comfortable she would be safe in a car. One eye was 20/40, the other 20/60, with the contacts she NEVER removed. (It remained the same for the rest of her life.) SHE NEVER COMPLAINED

Stacy began menstruating at age 14. This is normally a breeze, but not for her. She developed endometriosis. Her "periods" always came with pain and serious bleeding and clotting. She was put on birth control early to lessen the clotting and pain. I think that may have been her first dose of real pain. SHE NEVER COMPLAINED However, nobody mentioned one important fact: that you can get pregnant on birth control if you're also taking antibiotics.

When Stacy was 17 she had a bad attack of acute appendicitis and had to have an appendectomy, at the local hospital we came to despise.

I've been telling you all about her maladies, her difficulties. May I also let you know:

Stacy had a bevy of talents. She had a gifted voice and her ability to draw was exceptional. The first play she acted in was the King and I. She was 5. I will never forget that day as she walked off the stage, turned around and waved goodbye. The Director wasn't too happy. She auditioned for many parts, but these were usually met with brick walls. As an example, she was given a part in the production of "Wizard of Oz", but we had a Bar Mitzvah to attend that weekend. She was given the lead in the junior high school play but it was rescinded when they found out she was being "classified". This "classification" was because of her vision, but in addition, as we found out, the teachers didn't think she would be able to handle the lead as well as her schoolwork. I remember all the girls auditioning whispering, "Oh no, Stacy's auditioning." They knew they couldn't compete. And so she was crushed that she didn't get the part. The same thing happened when she auditioned for the "specialty "Arts" area high school. Another very big letdown. All because of the classification that I was talked into by the school Administration.

Stacy auditioned for the first season of "American Idol". She passed three levels and I was watching closely when 2 out of 3 judges wanted to move her ahead. But it took only one with a very big mouth to say no. So, after sleeping outside on the cement for two nights, she was cut. She continued to sing to students and at my school shows. She drew pictures for her students as well as her own children later on. She later made one video after another with her children and was asked to sing for a competition between bands on the "Opie and Anthony Show."

Stacy had such a HUGE personality that she was awarded "Best Sense Of Humor" in high school, edging slightly in front of one of her best friends Erika. There's always one person you'd meet in your lifetime that you never forgot. Stacy was THAT person. In fact, several months after her death I went to Atlantic City, (a place we would frequently take the kids), Harrah's Casino, and as uncanny as it may seem, a valet asked me how come my beautiful daughter was not with me. He also mentioned her beautiful children. It took me several minutes before I could tell him. He was visibly shocked and saddened. This was the effect she had on people. So beautiful, so friendly! She could imitate any dialect and often made videos sounding like certain famous actors. For her Bat Mitzvah project she asked to sing for the congregation, ("Yerushalaim") a song from "Schindler's List", however she never mentioned that she didn't know the words. The entire song was improvised with a "Yiddish/Hebrew" dialect. Most people didn't know the difference, but eyes were rolling between the Rabbi and Cantor.

For her last few years, Stacy slipped out of view from the general population. Only entering when forced to because she wanted people to remember her "The way she was" happy go-lucky, loving life, funny, and the "mom who went happily down the biggest slides, and rode the tallest waves". Something she used to enjoy with Cameron and Sierra before she became ill. However, she pushed herself to do everything while she was ill.

She consistently told me that "she didn't feel herself" That she felt "as if she was looking at the world from the outside"

She was the person you waited to arrive at all family gatherings. The one who constantly formulated unusual, fun games and events for her nieces and her own children to enjoy. She interacted and played with the kids from the moment she entered the house until the second she left. She didn't just do it. She got into it, she enjoyed it.

Stacy's relationship with each brother was special and different. Stacy and Randy were happy-go-lucky, playful and fun. Both had a little bit of "devil" inside. They double-dated and they partied heartily each watching and having the others back. Her relationship with Jeffrey was down-to-earth. She knew where to go when she needed sound advice and a level head. Jeffrey enjoyed her singing and cherished the birthday songs he received every year to his phone. But when it came to her sickness, she kept both brothers at Bay, hardly answering the phone, hardly making contact.

When Stacy was 21, she suffered a bad backwards fall. She herniated 5 discs and twisted her coccyx bone which actually hung by a thread for the rest of her life. She spent the next two years doing epidural injections. She had more than a dozen and eventually we found out that this probably had caused her arachnoiditis. When that didn't work, Stacy was given her first dose of pain medication. It was about this time that we noticed her feet were beginning to deform. I took her to two orthopedists who said she needed major foot surgery. This surgery, she said "was not going to happen right now." Unfortunately, it never did happen. SHE NEVER COMPLAINED

I enjoyed a very close relationship with my daughter. When Stacy turned 15, we began to take summer vacations together. We enjoyed a trip to California, driving from North to South, visiting with relatives and friends, while enjoying each other's company. One trip was with

Stacy's best friend Ivy and her Mom Gail, to the Dominican Republic and Canada. Had to watch those two with four eyes. They were severe boy magnets!! I enjoyed all our vacations together, but there were two that I will remember with the deepest of feelings. Our cruise to the Bahamas was very special. It was where I watched Stacy fall in love for the first time. But my favorite trip was with Cameron, Stacy's oldest son on a cruise to Bermuda. The photographer fell in love with him and followed him everywhere taking photos. We both thought she was a bit weird but at the end of the cruise she presented us with a portfolio of pictures which was stunning. A few years later, Cameron acquired a modeling contract, something his mother always wished she had done. On one occasion, a company asked for a mother to accompany a child. Stacy was pretty ill at the time, but it warmed my heart to see her fix her hair and pick out clothing and the amount of excitement that ran through her was electric. They were both excited to meet Morgan Freeman and Tia Leoni, and be on the set of Madam Secretary. Everybody on the set was so friendly and generous that they distributed the prizes in a carnival scene to the child actors.

While on birth control and antibiotics, Stacy became pregnant with her first child, whom she named Cameron. Because the coccyx bone was twisted inward, Cameron had to be delivered by C-section. At first glance, I knew an "angel" and a very special person was born that day. Stacy was ecstatic. She actually believed that she may not have been able to have children because of her endometriosis. Stacy was an excellent mother. Her rule was "No Hitting, No Screaming." If a child does something wrong, sit them down and explain the situation. If a child does something right, buy them a present!!

When Stacy was 26, she developed a hernia which was quickly repaired. Later on, she mentioned a few times that it felt like the mesh was protruding (she thought her body began to reject it). However, her surgeon felt it was fine. We never fully looked into it with the proper x-rays. My guess now, is that her body probably rejected all foreign substances.

Over the next few years Stacy developed three large ovarian cysts, one almost 10cm. They all had to be removed surgically and Stacy was told that she may not be able to produce any more children. My guess is that this is the reason she became pregnant for the second time: She wanted Cameron to have a sibling.

When Cameron was 3 years old, Stacy became pregnant with her daughter, whom she named Sierra; who also had to be delivered by C-Section. Throughout all of Stacy's medical problems, she had proven to be VERY fertile. Stacy believed in co-sleeping. Her belief was that sleeping with a parent led to confidence and strength. Stacy slept with Sierra until her death; Sierra was 6. She also breast-fed her until she was 4. Sierra called it "Num-Num". Through both pregnancies, Stacy was seen by a genealogist. We knew that Kevin's brother was challenged. We didn't know that Stacy had Homo-MTHFR mutation. But for Sierra, they said something was wrong. Even talked about aborting. When Stacy found out Sierra was a "daughter" I remember her saying "I will NEVER abort this baby". They thought Sierra was missing a chromosome. Sierra wasn't missing anything. The amnio proved she was perfect, like Cameron.

After Cameron was born, Stacy was eager to breast-feed. However, after only a few months she had taken ill and was forced to stop immediately. Because of the immediate stop, Stacy's breasts ended up looking like deflated balloons. They looked as if all muscle tissue was gone and the hanging skin affected her back problem. Stacy wanted to get implants. We argued for almost a year, but Stacy was determined to get her way, and she usually did. My sister mentioned that a major New York hospital had a "Mentoring Clinic", where an accredited Plastic Surgeon trained another one in their final year. The cost was considerably less, and I agreed to let it get done so as long as she got saline, not silicone. I had heard something about silicone implants that I wasn't comfortable with. Unfortunately, later on, we found out that silicone, not saline implants were used.

With a daughter and a son, Stacy developed a more mature personality. Eager and happy to raise her children. To teach them, nurture them and to give 100% of herself, and she did. Every part of her day was centered around her children. She never let them out of her sight, for even a minute. Yelling, punishing and hitting were prohibited. Her approach was loving, yet strong at teaching right from wrong. She made up her own games using themes of mystery and wonder. Her energy and determination lacked for nothing and she was known around two neighborhoods as the pied-piper who included everyone, not leaving anyone out.

On a quiet afternoon in January 2014 Stacy called me frantically screaming, "my legs, my legs, the pain"! Knowing my grandson had to be picked up from school, with phone in hand I don't know why I grabbed four ice packs (first aid training I guess) but I got into my car and raced the 15minute drive to her house. (in 8minutes) She was still screaming when I arrived. I applied the ice packs front and back, on her legs. I left to pick up Cameron from school and returned to the house. The pain had subsided by then. What in the world was that? We never really found out!

After this bout of initial pain in her legs, Stacy started to have similar, although lesser, twinges in her breasts and arms, but it was the legs that were always remembered. By March we had an appointment with my neurologist, Dr. F. He ordered first a CAT scan and an MRI; both were normal. A full round of blood work was done; it showed inflammation but nothing alarming. Next came an incident with swallowing, where food would get stuck in her throat and end up exiting her nose. Actually, it was noodles from a Campbells can of soup. She never had Campbell's chicken noodle soup again.

By April, the pains were becoming more frequent and in different parts of the arms and chest. On one particular day, Dr. F. suggested we meet him at the local hospital where he would perform a spinal tap. As Stacy and her father arrived at the ER, Dr. F. was called to an emergency and he instructed the ER Physician to begin the LP (BIG MISTAKE). This ER Physician stabbed Stacy 6 times before Dr. F. arrived; he noted on paper that Stacy was visibly traumatized. On his first tap, fluid was extracted and sent to the lab for testing. Other than rare lymphocytes (which we were told was blood probably from the botched tap) everything was normal. (This was reassuring; Stacy had thought she had ALS)

After the LP, Stacy developed a BAD spinal tap headache that just wouldn't go away. I brought her back to the hospital where they wanted to do a "blood patch", which puts back the blood into the many holes that have been made. I was dumbfounded, "You want to poke her again" and we left. After seven more days of suffering from mind blowing headaches, I took her to another physician. The blood patch was again suggested. WE ended up going back to the hospital because the headache was so debilitating, and this was the only suggestion to get rid of it. What they did ultimately was to take Stacy's blood from her body and put it into her spinal canal. Little did they know, (or inquire about the reason for the LP in the first place), they were taking that inflammatory blood from her body and putting it into her spine. After another week of having a mind-breaking headache, we went to Dr. Spiel, Stacy's former pain management physician, who then tried a second patch-once again taking the inflammatory blood from Stacy's body to put into her spine. After the 2nd blood patch was done, Stacy insisted that the headache had now turned into a HEAD PAIN that surpassed any pain she has ever felt, including the fall that twisted her coccyx bone or the C-sections of her children. AFTER THIS TIME, STACY NEVER STOPPED COMPLAINING OF HER HEAD PAIN.

I tried to get an appointment with a neurologist at a major teaching hospital in the area, but couldn't get one for two months. During this awful time, Stacy would be counting the hours until the head pain would abate. She would say, "Another day" another weekend, another month"! No! I can't take another minute. Mommy, please help me." Dr. Spiel suggested we go to their emergency room and try to get admitted that way. He told us of a "spectroscopy" brain test that was better than an MRI. We mentioned it to the emergency room physician and they did not know of it. At the emergency room, we tried for hours to get through to Dr. Spiel. Finally after four hours, the Doctors spoke and it was agreed that Stacy would be admitted in order to take this test. To make a long story short, it was "flu season" and Stacy's two year old would not be allowed on the patient floor. I remember the emergency room being filthy and full of patients everywhere.

I would not leave my daughter and she was still nursing. I ended up sleeping on the couches downstairs in the lobby with Sierra for four nights. I tried my hardest to make it fun for Sierra. I took her to the park. I took her to the children's library where they gave her gifts. I took her to the gift shop where I bought her gifts. I went home, got Cameron and brought him back so he could see his mother. I took Sierra to a local park. But Stacy never was given the test. Every day was a different excuse; The machine was in the other building. The machine is coming tomorrow. We don't have the machine, period! The beginning of awful hospital visits.

We then got a prescription from Dr. F. for the "Spectroscopy" and had it done at St. Peter's Hospital. I usually wait a day or two, then begin to look for test results; however, the next day we were called and were told they somehow lost the imaging and we would have to go repeat the test again. I remember playing with Cameron with a pull-back toy from McDonalds I had put into my purse. We always tried to make the medical visits fun for the kids. And Stacy always did. I wasn't as creative as she was. After both tests, it also did not show anything. When the head pain didn't subside, we looked for other options to rid her of this debilitating pain. Her brother Randy found Dr. L. at a major hospital in North Carolina. She was a specialist into LP closings and head pressure. I was in touch with Dr. L. three times and canceled her appointments as well because I had to be convinced she wouldn't again use Stacy's inflamed blood and close it in there with Fibrin glue. When I got that assurance in a phone conversation with her, we decided to fly to North Carolina with Stacy's three year old daughter Sierra and have the procedure. However, Dr. L. did in fact, use a portion of her blood and combined it with fibrin glue and locked it in. Of course we had an argument, of course she apologized. Again, what good did that do! The inflamed blood was locked into her spine.

Kevin drove down to meet us in North Carolina three days later and we all drove home, very upset. This was a major turning point for Stacy as she began to lose hope in ridding herself of this unmanageable head pain. And we were also dealing with the realization that something was very wrong with the medical community.

One of the best suggestions I had gotten was from my cousin, Mark. Dr. Mark suggested keeping a log detailing her medical history to date and an introduction letter from her main physician. And to keep that log with me at all times. I updated it continually, because Stacy wanted this book to be written someday. Because of that suggestion, I have the information from every single visit with the hopes that nobody else would have to experience the trauma of what Stacy went through.

Stacy's dad found Dr. P., an interventional physician. He did a lot of tests and this is where we found out that Stacy had the homozygous mutated MTHFR gene. This gene had caused Stacy not to be able to expel the toxins from her breast implants from her body fast enough. This gene probably caused Stacy to reject that first DPT inoculation and also caused the nystagmus. This gene was a nightmare for her. It is also believed that this mutated gene made it twice as hard to get rid of the benzos and opioids, making the withdrawals longer and more painful. He found the root of the problem but was incapable of helping cure it.

Stacy became annoyed when neurologists would tell her she probably had migraines as she tried to explain to them that her head pain hadn't subsided or changed in years. But after months of arguing, Stacy relented and allowed me to schedule an appointment with a neurologist/migraine specialist at another major New Jersey hospital. I knew she didn't have migraines, however I thought that if her present medication wasn't able to cross the blood/brain barrier, maybe a "migraine specialist" had something that would. This may have been the worst neurological appointment ever. This man was so nasty and short-tempered that even his assistant tried to speak over him. We left again, disappointed and kept shaking our heads. We didn't look at one another or speak the entire way home.

Soon after our trip to North Carolina, Stacy began to realize that her breasts were lopsided. Difficult to tell because she was still nursing. We made an appointment with her gynecologist and he couldn't tell either. He suggested she see a plastic breast surgeon. Dr. Z. suggested her breast implant may have leaked. I got in touch with the hospital where Stacy had received her implants and was stunned to hear that she had silicone rather than saline which I was sure we had asked for. I cried immediately at the news, phone in hand. Then the research began and everything made more sense. Within three weeks I was able to secure an appointment with the leading physician in the field of "Breast Implant Disease", Doctor. Susan Kolb in Atlanta. We chose Doctor Kolb over all the others because of her expertise in detoxing the body. We were fortunate that she had a cancellation and scheduled Stacy to explant her implants, and begin ridding her body of the toxins which by this time had run rampant in her body. Off to Atlanta, Stacy, Sierra and I. The procedure was no picnic. Stacy cried for three days. She also ended up back in the emergency room with pain and bleeding. I really liked Atlanta. There was a carnival going on and I took Sierra there every night. I found a beautiful park that had a huge food fair and little streams. I took Stacy there before we left for home. Right before leaving Atlanta, I took a picture of a billboard sign that read "Everything will be OK". I pointed it out to her. I'd hoped and prayed it to be true.

In June of 2017, Stacy had her implants removed and sent to be tested by Dr. Blais in Canada. Dr. Blais reported her implants being the worst defective implants he had ever seen, coming from different lots and should never have been placed into the public for sale. However, after reading his report and noticing it didn't mention the word "leak," the family again became skeptical of her illness. Thus being the start of her distancing herself from her family. Dr. Kolb took out many infected lymph nodes as well. She was great in educating Stacy about supplements, nutrition, and detox. We purchased supplements and spent thousands of dollars over the course of treatment, hoping it would eventually begin to heal her body, but unfortunately it didn't. Dr. Kolb was always available to us and answered any questions emailed to her immediately for the next three years. A suggestion from a friend, a registered nurse suggested we try a local Chinese healing store. It had worked for them, why not Stacy. I spent over $500 there. It did not work for Stacy!! I purchased the "harmonic quad" for over $300. It was a machine that was supposed to help dispel the toxins and ultimately kill any parasites that had formed. It didn't work either. It has been since taken off the market.

Also in June 2017, I contacted the FDA to inform them of Dr. Kolbs findings and filled out a complaint form against the silicone implants manufacturer, Allergan. Three years later, in May 2020, I contacted them to see why I hadn't received any response and initially was told I'd have to pay for a report on their findings. I'd gladly pay for the report, but why wait three years and not contact the individual? In June 2020 they finally told me that Stacy's brand of implants are not scheduled at this time to be removed from purchase. In 2017 Stacy contacted everybody from her Breast Implants website. What we found out was shocking, to say the least. Several years ago in 2008, there were thousands of terrified sick women who complained to the FDA. Eventually they took the implants off of the market. The courts were then flooded with lawsuits. An individual cannot sue the manufacturing companies until the implants are deemed not fit for purchase by the FDA. In 2019, a brand different from Stacy's (ribbed implants were removed from the market). We've contacted many attorneys and could not secure one to take her case until the FDA removed Stacy's implants from the market. We found out that France removed implants from their country and even paid for the women to have them taken out. We were told of shocking stories of bullying and threats to many individuals, (including physicians) who advocated against breast implants. This was a quest for Stacy as she wanted someone to pay for what was done to her. Again, a very bad stain on the medical community, as Physicians continue to implant these women without educating them on the risks.

After Stacy healed from the surgery, it was apparent that she wasn't getting better. That's when we were told she should try "chelation, " a process that removes heavy metals from the body. We were stunned to find out that "silicone implants" were made with such dangerous chemicals such as arsenic, lead, titanium, cadmium, and many others. I am a Health teacher and remember the same shock when learning about the ingredients in cigarettes. She also started supplements such as inositol to try to rid the body of the silicone. Along with chelation, Stacy was also given doses of IV vitamins. Dr. Kolb suggested "foot baths" to assist in ridding her body of the toxins. All of these suggestions DID help her body, not cure it, but her HEAD PAIN NEVER subsided.

Soon after explanting her breast implants, Stacy began noticing a weird dermatological presence on her skin. Her face and shoulders presented a sort of living substance that came out of her pores. She swore they moved, they hurt. Some were hard like nails, some had shape. She then developed large bumps that also hurt. I then took her to a fair amount of dermatologists, including our own family Dermatologist who I thought was the smartest man on earth. I said to Stacy, "Dr. H.will know what it is", and infectious disease physicians in both New York and New Jersey who all but told her she was crazy. I even had the bumps tested by an oncologist. Along with the strange skin problem, she noticed a red thread-like substance on her pants a number of times (all over her pants) and a black line that filled in the lines on the inside of her palms. I have photos of all of these. It was suggested that this may be Morgellons Disease. Dr. Kolb, however, mentioned she thought Stacy had chemical parasites. Our insurance company allowed one round of Albenza for the parasites, then refused any prescriptions from Dr. Kolb, who was out of Atlanta. We then got the Albenza from Canada. The skin problem improved but never totally disappeared. During this time, it was suggested the use of the hyperbaric chamber might help Stacy's body heal. I was about to meet with the executives from our local hospital to plead the case for use of this machine when Dr. Kolb suggested that if Stacy did have parasites, this would give them Oxygen and they would overtake the body. We gave up the idea to use the chamber.

The "parasites," (something we never got clinically diagnosed), absolutely drove Stacy so insane that she stole over 200 Ativan pills from her father which landed her in The Silver Hill Hospital for detox. Silver Hill, however switched her from detox and placed her in their chronic pain section along with giving her a "scholarship" because that's where they felt she best belonged; in chronic pain. At Silver Hill she wrote a beautiful letter that I'd like to share with you about "PAIN":

Dear Pain,

I was so happy with my life before you. I spoke about how lucky I was that I was given two beautiful healthy children. I was Supermom. I carried my babies throughout amusement parks on my hip for hours. I took them for races up hills and went down that same hill in the snow.

But then you struck me with an illness that so few doctors knew about. I remember how you arrived after a family flu. You began giving me pain in my legs, so bad I had to call for help. After that, so many different symptoms. You made my hands, feet and breasts burn. Along with that, the terrible feeling of helplessness which caused anxiety.

YOU increased after the spinal tap gone wrong, but tripled after the blood patches. The head pain was the worst, giving me popping, crackling sounds and tremendous PAIN.

Many doctors later, we found out my silicone breast implants were defective and leaking. So, PAIN-you made me leave my 6-year old son for two weeks to remove them.

My 2-year old daughter had to watch me scream in PAIN after surgery, as she was crying for her milk. Then detox began. Enormous amounts of pills and bills.

Seven months later' PAIN-you are still in my head, back and feet. The Oxycodone I took for a previous accident began not to work, so I started doubling up on the Ativan. Pain-you were so bad.

doctors still do not know what is wrong with my head.

PAIN-you turned me from a happy, relaxed mother with no worries to someone who worries 24/7, about my babies and my family. Still don't know what is going to be, still scared, but the love for my kids strengthens me to say that I will defeat YOU for I am a Mother and I am a survivor.

Written by Stacy Shain

At Silver Hill, true to her personality, Stacy made a lot of friends. She breezed through there helping as many people as she could. Everyone loved her, patients as well as staff. Before departing, she sang in their talent show and looked forward to reuniting with her children. When Stacy returned home, a "friend" from Silver Hill contacted her. She wanted to come visit. On her visit, she asked Stacy to cash a check for her. Stacy didn't have enough in her account, so the "friend" wrote two checks and the bank held one against Stacy's account and one against mine (even though the accounts weren't connected). Of course the checks bounced. I tried to get the money back, even called her parents. I got only the money taken from my account. An expensive lesson learned!

Silver Hill set Stacy up with a psychiatrist in the Jackson, N.J. area. On Stacy's first visit with him, I sat to first explain Stacy's Medical problems. He seemed oblivious as to why Stacy was sent to him. This was a perfect prelude to what Stacy was to experience for the rest of her life. Dr. C. cut Stacy's daily benzo medication from 4 pills to 3 on that first visit. Silver Hill had explained to us that it was important for a patient to be on an "even keel" and Stacy went into an immediate withdrawal.

I put three calls into the office and never got a call back from anyone. Most of the time, I would get only a voicemail. Stacy continued to sweat, twitch and experience signs of benzo withdrawal. I was able to receive a call back when I said I wanted to make an appointment. At her next appointment, Dr. C. said that Stacy's problem was "medical" and that he wasn't equipped to help her. We were terrified that she had a medical problem that would never be resolved. I called Silver Hill and never got a call back. In fact, throughout the next two years, I called Silver Hill a few times and never got a call back. I heard: Once you leave them, they leave you as well.

I tried to find a psychiatrist, but the waiting list was either too long or they didn't accept any insurance, or they just weren't accepting new patients. Randy suggested I try his medical professional. We made an appointment and sat in the waiting room for over two hours. The Physician refused to write a prescription and I left to take the kids into the car. When Stacy came out, she was crying. She told me he said "The only way you'll ever find out if there's silicone in your brain is through an autopsy when you die" Not only was that a terrible thing to say to an already traumatized sick individual, it was untrue. Silicone is not easily recognized or diagnosed.

Luckily, Dr. F. was willing to write the Ativan until a psychiatrist was secured. To think a psychiatrist would just dismiss a patient on medication without a course to secure medication first, was so unprofessional. To cut a complete pill and not do it slowly was cruel as well. The cruelest part was knowing that they knew the patient would withdraw but just didn't care.

Stacy remained on the Suboxone and Ativan for the next six months; however she began to get sicker. She began to have problems regulating body heat. She was mostly cold. She would walk around daily with heating pads on her arms and legs. She said the shower and bath water began to sting her skin. She had diarrhea more often. There were increased problems swallowing along with possible thyroid problems. This was in addition to her head pain, that NEVER went away. The diarrhea came more often and she began to lose control of her bowels. She would give me her clothing to wash as she was embarrassed to place it in the family hamper. Her hands were beginning to disfigure, looking more and more arthritic, her feet got worse and the shaking became constant.

The diarrhea, along with the inability to eat caused her to lose quite a bit of weight. She hovered around 95-100 lbs. A colonoscopy showed that she had chronic colitis. Her appetite was irrational. She would have bouts of eating ferociously, then would not eat for days. She was hungry but she couldn't handle the diarrhea. Her Gastroenterologist prescribed Viberzi and a good probiotic but the Viberzi was not recommended for long term use. She would use Viberzi and Imodium. It became part of her diet. Her shopping list for me would consist daily of Vanilla Swiss Almond Hagan-Daz, muffins, and red bull. (along with Imodium). As I walk through the supermarkets now, glancing at these items, would cause me to break out in tears.

My husband suggested I take her to HIS gastroenterologist. He had a lot of faith in him. The Doctor was-backlogged for over an hour. Inside his room he asked, and Stacy answered all his questions, then excused himself. In the hallway, we overheard him say to his patient across from us. "I'm going to be a little late. have a woman in there, well, you know how they can be." Stacy got up and walked out. End of that appointment.

Eventually, Stacy was told she was hypoglycemic. After a big meal she would begin to fall asleep sitting up at the table. People were thinking she wasn't taking her medication correctly. She was constantly trying to explain herself. At her favorite restaurant, they brought her a cup of coffee with an extra shot of caffeine, no charge! She was grateful. KLEINS OF BELMAR, THE BEST; HER FAVORITE.

Another major problem was the inability to sleep. She was exhausted but wanted to do everything for her children. So, she would either drink coffee or Red Bull. She could not mix a sleeping pill with her Valium so it wasn't prescribed. She was always tired, worn out and in PAIN.

During this time we secured an appointment with Dr. L., rheumatologist. I say it this way because Dr. L. would not see Stacy while she was on pain medication. After Silver Hill and on Suboxone, an appointment was given.

Dr. L. was overwhelmed with Stacy's condition, and the constant negativity from his office assistant was disheartening. She would always enter and declare that he was taking too much time with Stacy. Dr. L. knew that Stacy needed to be on pain medication but he was not happy writing it. He would grit his teeth and sometimes raise his voice to the point that Stacy did not want to go to an appointment without me. He seemed very interested in her case and interacting with different "executives", we had secured in this field.

I contacted The Mayo Clinic for an appointment with a neurologist, had all her records sent, only to be rejected for an appointment. To even do this, I had to request files from all of her doctors. It took weeks to get a return from all of them and then send to Mayo Clinic.

They said they couldn't help her! Soon, her doctors began charging to copy records.

I contacted Johns Hopkins for an appointment with a neurologist, had all her records sent, only to be rejected for an appointment. One day I gathered up Stacy and Sierra and drove the three hours to Baltimore to try and get into Johns Hopkins through the ER. We waited in the waiting room for 7 hours. They ended up admitting her but the neurologist who treated her was also teaching a class. He took such a hard, cold approach that even one of the students apologized for his actions when they left. I slept on a couch for three days in her room while she nursed her daughter, who was two years old at the time. and the only test done on her brain was an MRI. Again, so very disappointing!!

We were able to get an appointment with the Cleveland Clinic. Again, after taking weeks to secure all of Stacy's records, an appointment was made. You don't get to choose a doctor. You have to rely on who they best think you should see. So after driving seven hours in the snow, with Stacy and Sierra, I prayed they would give us a long awaited miracle. However medically qualified this doctor was, he was not the right one for Stacy. His specialty lied in the "epilepsy field". Why the intake person felt Stacy needed an "epilepsy appointment", I still do not know. Something is very wrong with our medical community.

It was suggested that I try the Undiagnosed Division of the NIH. To do this, I had to figure out what research segments they were working on and where Stacy would best fit in. I sent in all Stacy's records and we drove to West Virginia with Stacy, Sierra, Cameron, Dad and I. The NIH was a massive beautiful complex. They didn't charge us and housed us in beautiful quarters. Dad took Cameron to Washington while I stayed with Sierra and Stacy. They had a beautiful children's complex where Sierra would play while Stacy was being tested. They tested Stacy for their research which proved negative and gave her a simple MRI. Stacy was under their care for five days. Unfortunately, this visit too, was unproductive for Stacy.

You see, Stacy had a head pain that wasn't showing up on any imaging, so nobody wanted to take the time to find out what was causing it.

During the next year Stacy saw Dr. G. Temple University Neurology, Dr. C. at RWJ Neurology, Dr. K. at Columbia Neurology and Dr. N. At Lenox Hill Neurology. She saw two Neurosurgeons who all but thought we were crazy for making an appointment. Stacy found a neurologist in Cape May, N.J., a two hour drive south with a specialty (from his website) in neuro-inflammation. However, when we met him, he offered no insight on the problem Stacy was having. I even contacted a former relative who has been divorced from my husband's cousin for more than 25 years. He is a Neurosurgeon and I was hoping he would take a personal interest. He didn't! We began looking for specialty tests other than CTs and MRI's. Stacy found something done with water and she took that special test, from a special friend who is an interventional Radiologist. However, it also didn't show anything.

Stacy found a neurologist in Northern NJ who listed "Toxic Neurological Problems" on his website. She called this time to make sure the trip wouldn't be wasted on another "idiot". Cameron, her son begged to take off from school to meet the man who would help his mother. This guy was the worst!!! Cold, calculating and again a waste of time. I'll never forget leaving the office and Cameron saying, "What a jerk"!

Through research, I found Dr. W., a neurologist who ran a clinic in California. Dr. W. was able to take the spinal fluid and test it for any "foreign bodies". I tried my damned hardest to get her spinal fluid to him but there were roadblocks all throughout the process. It seemed that Dr. W. clinic wanted the receiving hospital who had taken the fluid to pay for the research. We offered to pay directly. We offered to give the money in advance to the hospital. I went to all the hospitals in the area and nobody would do it. Dr. W. also wanted to use the spinal fluid for research purpose and this scared off the hospitals. I got Dr. Mark , a physician in California, to intervene. He also tried and failed. I almost made reservations to fly to Calif, however I needed to speak to Dr. Wilson to set up the timing with Stacy's children and school and Dr. Wilson never returned my calls. Dr. F., Stacy's local neurologist, actually spoke to Dr. W. and advised us cautiously on pursuing this course of action because Dr. W. told him that silicone and parasites may not show up in his research of Stacy's spinal fluid. Still, if Dr. W. would've returned my call, we would have taken the chance and that flight to California. I would've gone anywhere. I would've done anything for my daughter.

During a sunny day in September 2017, Stacy found Dr. N. on her own. A movie was made about him helping a girl with autoimmune issues. Stacy was hoping she could be that girl; however, Dr. N. didn't believe she had autoimmune disease. Again, we contacted Dr. Kolb who explained that "The Breast Illness" disease mimics many autoimmune diseases. For example, Stacy's blood tests showed thyroid problems, yet the specialist said her thyroid was OK. Stacy's blood tests showed possible scleroderma, yet the scleroderma specialists said she did not in fact have it. We saw Dr. N. four times. On our first visit, he told Sierra, "I will make your Mommy all better". I truly believed that if Dr. N. took the time, he would've been able to figure out how to help her. Stacy insisted we watch the movie about him and we did. During our last visit, Dr. N. said they were coming out soon with new imaging and he would contact us when it became available. That was like a "Don't call us, we'll call you" goodbye! Dr. N. was the only specialist I contacted about Stacy's death. Sierra wrote a letter to him detailing his broken promise of "making my Mom better" and that, "you should listen, really listen" to your patients. And because he didn't, she didn't have a Mommy anymore.

Even though Stacy had always sent the kids off with lunchbox notes, as she began to get more and more frightened, she started slipping love notes daily into the kids lunch. It was a practice she actually remembered I had done. For her, it had a different meaning. It was something she wanted to leave her children if something was to happen to her. A few times she hadn't been able to wake up and put the note in and she was visibly upset. I would drive to the school and hand it to them During this time, Cameron's teacher Mrs. Z. took it upon herself to call DYFUS, claiming Stacy sounded "too needy". DYFUS showed up to the house. Stacy was embarrassed, insulted and taken aback. DYFUS apologized, saying it was their job to make contact when a complaint was placed, but closed the file that very day. At a time where parents are abusing their children, and Stacy being ill, making her love notes look trashy was like a "slap in the face" to her. We made an appointment and aired our views with the Superintendent. He was appalled as well, admitting that HIS wife also put notes into his own children's lunch boxes. After a meeting with the principal and teacher, an apology was given to Cameron, none to Stacy. The children will always have this very special folder, with all of Stacy's notes.

Stacy was excited when she saw a new television show that was about to be aired. It was a new "diagnostic" medical show called "chasing the cure". I filled out all the paperwork, and contacted the show several times. Unfortunately, Stacy was not chosen (and the show has since been cancelled)

It was about this time that I began to get more and more terrified of not being able to help my daughter. I began to write to Politicians for help. I received return letters but in the end I received no help. I wrote to the President, Governor and Senator. I actually walked into my Congressman's office to complain about the opioid crisis and how my daughter needed her medication. They responded that they would intervene, if necessary, if she couldn't get her medication. I must say on behalf of our Insurance company, Aetna, Supervisor Mary was THE BEST. She never let us down when there was a problem.

Stacy began to search more and more frantically for a cure. She was on her phone constantly. She had a one track mind on her medical treatment, and that was how she searched for her miracle. She wholeheartedly believed there was something in her head; either a parasite or "silicone". She also believed that her body needed "opioids" in order to survive. She believed that her personality was changing, and this was very important to her. If you argued this point with her, you were dismissed. Our arguments were about her taking care of her body, while we searched for someone to fix her head pain. She stopped taking her supplements, saying four years was enough and felt they weren't helping and destroying her stomach. She didn't eat healthfully, nor did she do any exercise. I tried Physical Therapy with her twice and that was a simple disaster. They actually didn't know what to do with her. After a while, I was only too happy to see her eat anything as she became dangerously thin. Unfortunately, we began to argue and sadly, I am left with the memory of those arguments.

Soon after that last appointment with Dr. N., she left to go to the store. After 40 minutes I began wondering where she was. I began calling, no answer. I put the phone on redial and called non-stop and she finally answered. What she said, sent chills down my spine causing me to gather the kids and get into my car. I really didn't know where I was going. She said, "I love you, make sure you always tell my kids I love them". I tried calling again, no answer. Cameron said "give me your phone"-he texted her. He said "this is Cameron, pick up the phone". She picked it up and said "I love you Cameron," and hung up. I called the police. Cameron said: "Maybe there's a tracker on her phone, call Dad". I did and there was. I found her sitting in her car, parked. I made her open the door. She said, "I don't want to be like this anymore". Then I saw the cuts on her wrist. The police arrived. They took her to the local hospital, where they put her in a light blue room with a bed in the middle, no sheet. She told them she had a fight with her boyfriend and she was upset over it. I called a girlfriend of mine in California. She put together a three-way call with a "spiratual healer" she had taken a class with. He told Stacy by the time the conversation was finished she would be cured. This may have been the most ridiculous thing I have ever witnessed. Stacy rolled her eyes at me. My girlfriend apologized. The hospital discharged her believing her story. I however, did not. I looked up stress and depression and was connected with a group that worked with our local trauma hospital. I immediately took her there. When the intake woman saw the cuts, she called the police, who then escorted her to the hospital.

At the hospital, I told them I had Power of Attorney over her medical situation and they told me they were admitting her into a program that would help her. A program that would counsel her and treat her depression. I was not allowed to talk to anyone and nobody would talk to me. The program they described turned out to be full of Heroin addicts who had overdosed. The counseling consisted of group sessions and no individualized sessions related to drug overdosing. The physician in charge was full speed forward on taking away all of my daughter's medication. They drugged her up so much that she didn't leave her bed for two days. When she did, others on the floor said to her; "we were wondering when you would appear". Only then was she seen by pain management, who, in fact, had a loud argument with the psychiatrist that was loud enough for the whole floor to hear. Again, pain management insisted Stacy needed to be on "pain medication". One of Stacy's nurses admitted she also had fibromyalgia and fought for Stacy to keep them from dropping her pain medication so soon. I was not allowed to see her for three days. When I did, Stacy said plainly, "Mom this is not the place for me. They want to take all my meds away and they are doing it way too quickly. I'm sicker than I ever was". I tried to speak to the psychiatrist, but I never got to until Stacy was discharged. He was too "busy" to speak to me. I took her home on the fifth day. At discharge, the psychiatrist called my daughter an "addict" and Stacy educated him loudly. She said: "An addict is a person who takes drugs for fun. I take it because I need it to function on an everyday basis". She absolutely hated when doctors combined the two! She was a strong advocate for chronic pain patients, belonging to a website that shared similar horror stories to her own. She also belonged to the website that advocated for the women of breast implant disease.

The only two tests that proved positive were the ones finalized later on with Dr. K., from Columbia University showing she had small fiber neuropathy. A disease with no cure. A disease that takes away the safety bonding we have around our nerve cells, which explained the deregulation of body temperature. Stacy had a VERY bad case and was told she needed to seek out good pain management. The same thing was told to us when the "fibromyalgia" test was finalized. Stacy's numbers were in the high 90's on both tests. It was about this time, her neck began to hurt intensely, as well as her feet. It also became very clear that she was having trouble walking. I made another appointment with the foot doctor. A few months later, and with her new medical conditions, Stacy's pain level began to rise. Dr. Furman wrote a prescription for Tylenol with Codeine. She tried this for two months. It was not enough. He then tried Percocet twice daily. He then raised it to four times daily. Refusing to be a pain management physician for her, he then turned it over to Dr. L. Dr. L. first tried oxycodone 10mg twice daily for a few months, then 10mg 4 times daily. I won't bore you with the short of it. Her medication was changed every few months and her final dose of opioid medication was a fentanyl patch of 150mg every 48 hours.

At first, we tried everything Dr. Kolb suggested. I hired a nurse to administer massage therapy twice a week for a few months, even purchasing special pain-relieving cream. We tried CBD and marijuana. After a while, Stacy said the cream burned her skin and refused the massages. Dr. F. wrote a prescription for physical therapy and chiropractic appointments. She fought this as well. But to her credit, she did try it. When it didn't help, she refused to continue.

It was around this time that the Nation had declared a "war on opioids". They were making it very difficult for the doctors to write a prescription. The paperwork was collectively unbelievable. Along with the Nation's "war on Opioids", I was fighting my family's war on opioids.

They also believed that Stacy should wean off all of her medications. Dr. L. was not a pain management specialist and we contacted Dr. Spiel who was Stacy's former pain management physician (who was doing only stem cell transplants at this time) but was nice enough to give his opinion. We were also in contact with Dr. Forest Tennent out of California, who was nice enough to test Stacy for arachnoiditis and speak to Dr. L. about his course of treatment. I also took Stacy to the Johns Hopkins Blaustein Pain Management Center where Dr. E. also agreed that Stacy needed to be on opioids, mainly because her condition was NOT curable, nor was it going to get better. I actually took Stacy to four local pain management specialists, all of whom refused to write a prescription at the end of the appointment. Which landed us back to Dr. L.

Another incident Stacy had with medication was when Dr. L. went on vacation/Sabbatical overseas and forgot to leave a prescription for her and she ran out of medication. Nobody would write one for her. At that time she was on oxycodone and valium. We eventually realized that the only way Stacy could get medication was to go to the C. Clinic and get Suboxone. When I called the Clinic I told them I didn't want them to touch her Valium, they agreed, however as soon as we got there and I left, they put her on a very low dose of Subutex and changed her to a low dose of Klonopin. Now Klonopin is already less effective than Valium and the dose of Subutex was so low that she began to withdraw. The admitting Doctor told us he had to follow the clinic's protocol, even though he didn't agree with it. Stacy's treating physician at carrier suggested I take her elsewhere. Elsewhere? We were running out of elsewhere. Stacy spent all five days there crying. The day after she left Carrier, I took her to the Blaustein center at Johns Hopkins and Dr. Erdek spoke to Dr. L. They agreed to have her try the Dilaudid pills and placed her back on Valium. The Dilaurdid, in pill form was not sufficient for her level of pain and was soon back on Fentanyl Patches. Please keep in mind, none of these pain relievers helped her HEAD PAIN.

Unfortunately, Stacy had yet another "medication" incident. I picked up Stacy's medication one day and checked the labels as I usually do. A few days later, she began to complain of withdrawal symptoms. At first, I didn't believe her. Until I saw her sweat and shake. With a magnifying glass, Stacy looked directly at the pill and noticed the Valium given to her was half the dose. I actually took it into CVS to make sure. I could not believe it! The Pharmacy we used for over three years had put the wrong dose pill in the bottle labeling it with the correct dose. All I got was a "were sorry". I wanted to switch pharmacies, but Stacy did not want herself to be labelled "a Pharmacy hopper", so we stayed. However, in two weeks when I went to retrieve her Fentanyl patches and was told they didn't have any, I was livid. No warning and left without any means to purchase such a strong medication. We switched Pharmacies. I'm assuming the paperwork became too much for them, and they didn't want to deal with it.

In June of 2018, for my sister's 70th birthday, we went to Florida. Stacy, Kevin and the kids, her brother Randy and his family, and me. First stop was a huge party, and Stacy was extremely uncomfortable. I talked her into having her hair done professionally. She looked beautiful, but terribly thin. Afterwards we drove to Disney, one of Stacy's favorite places. Her pharmacist would not issue her medication two days early and my husband had to pay more than $100 to have it shipped the next day to the hotel. Sierra was having a urinating problem, going to the bathroom every half hour. Stacy would have to get off lines to take her to the bathroom. She carried her all throughout the park. I made sure she had water bottles full of liquids, so she would not overheat from the high temperatures. At one point, in the middle of a long line, she almost passed out. She was trapped within a long line forgetting to take her water bottle. Little did we know, Stacy was two months pregnant at the time. At dinnertime, it all probably hit her at once and she sat on the ground and cried. She was upset that her favorite place now became a damaged memory for her.

After returning from Florida, Stacy's teeth began to hurt her. I made an appointment with our dentist, who said she needed to see a periodontist. The periodontist explained that she needed extensive periodontal work on her gums. Her gums were beginning to recede. We began to research and found out that this was also a side effect of chemical toxicity. At the news, Stacy's face turned white, as her teeth were always particularly important to her. Her smile, she was told many millions of times over, was totally radiant. (Unfortunately, with pregnancy and illness, the work never got done)

In Sept 2018, after finding out she was Pregnant instead of the usual excited feeling, I noticed she was worried and scared. Basically, she was in shock because she was actually almost 7 months pregnant. As she was so thin, we were both in shock. The pregnancy and delivery were not easy for her, yet her strength, physically and mentally, was incredible. She began to get chest palpitations and it was suggested that they try to wean her off the Fentanyl, and she agreed for the sake of the baby. She was placed in the hospital for five days and they tried to do just that, lower her medications. However, at this time we were shocked to discover that the major hospital in our area (a teaching hospital), does not employ a pain management team who would agree to care for pregnant women. Stacy had to rely on the hospital's psychiatric department to issue her medication. They just could not come up with the correct dose and she began withdrawing. Dr. L. had come to visit and ended up placing her back on the fentanyl patch, again for the sake of the baby. Even after Dr. L. had remained for two hours to write out a prescription, the attending physician left for home before submitting it and Stacy went the entire night WITHOUT any medication, the palpitations, sweating and pain steadily increased. At this point she was petrified as to what was to become of her during the delivery. Dr. Rosen, chief of the high-risk pregnancy division discussed the importance of Stacy having her tubes tied. She would not make that decision until they wheeled her in for delivery. Dr. Rosen was fearful of another pregnancy, given her overall medical condition. The delivery was so hard on her already traumatized body. Coming out of the delivery room she was covered by multiple heated blankets so that only her face was showing. Another procedure done on her in the delivery room was by a plastic surgeon, as she was too thin for him to suture her in the usual way. She had something of a tummy tuck performed. I would like to add that I stayed with Stacy non-stop for the first three days and I held and fed Jax who was absolutely perfect in my eyes. I still believe that because Stacy was on opioids, they put Jax into ICU for no reason other than "the opioid scare". He would not drink the Similac, however Stacy mustered up the strength to go nurse him and pump. He DID drink her breast milk. As far as Stacy's medication. I believe for the first time since she got ill, they overdid it, then sent in a social worker and asked me to leave despite Stacy's asking if I could stay. (Because she was groggy and very well medicated). Next thing we find out a report against Stacy was written. An employee had to remain in the room around the clock (along with me) and plastic silverware was delivered. All because Stacy was taking "opioids". Later, a social worker would arrive at her home. Case was again closed.

The worst incident Stacy had with her medication was right after her birthday in July. I drove Stacy and her three children to Niagara Falls, wanting to make it a special birthday for her. Stacy tried hard to make this a fun vacation for the kids. She stood outside, and they all got soaked on the "Maid of The Mist", while I stayed inside with the baby. She walked up and down the steepest hills. She enjoyed signature Starbuck specialties. She played games and did her magic at the prize counter, at a three-floor indoor arcade. We had dinner atop the famous Skylon Towers seafood buffet, where, when evening comes, you can see all of Niagara Falls illuminated. She watched as Sierra and Cameron were airlifted inside an air chamber, thinking whether she could do it. I wanted her to try, to have some fun, but she refused. The second night, however, she became ill-and wound up having double pneumonia as well as shingles. Cameron looked at me at 4 in the morning and said, "Is there a hospital nearby?" I said pack it up!

And we drove back to New Jersey.

I immediately dropped the children off and headed to the local emergency room. At the triage I told them I had Power of Attorney over Stacy's medical. She was extremely sick, but she began speaking about what was wrong, I finished. Inside the emergency room, we both spoke. I again told them I had Power of Attorney and nothing was to be given to her without my permission. I had her files with me, and I told them she was a chronic pain patient. Stacy asked me to get her things out of the car, as she would be sleeping over. By the time I came back, they had given her Narcan. Seems the emergency room personnel told the admitting physician on the 2nd floor that Stacy was on a fentanyl patch and "out of it," so he ordered the Narcan without even examining her. This act put her into an immediate withdrawal. So, in addition to her original medical problems, shingles AND pneumonia, she had to fight the immediate withdrawal caused by Narcan. She never really got over that incident. All my complaints fell on deaf ears. And they forced us to continue with the doctor who ordered it as there was not another one to tend to her. To make matters worse, they stupidly left on the fentanyl patch, so she continued to feel the symptoms of immediate withdrawal!

Stacy was visibly shaken after this incident and became more depressed. She spent most of August in the house with the kids. She steadily began to withdraw, only speaking to family and friends through texting or Facebook. She did, however, venture out once. After bringing her three dresses to choose from for her brothers upcoming wedding, she asked to be taken to the store to pick one of her choosing. She chose a beautiful blue sequined dress and asked me to take a picture and show it to Alli (her sister-in-law), to get her opinion. I asked her several times what song she would sing at her Jeffrey's wedding, as she had sung for her other brother Randy. Sierra kept saying that mommy was going to sing "Baby Shark" I knew she was going to sing "Shallow" from "A Star Is Born," as she watched the movie a few times. After the movie, she asked for me to tell Dr. B. that she had no problem formulating "tears", something he said she did not have at their appointment.

By the end of August 2019, I felt I had to do something drastic. My husband and I finally agreed to take her to Dr. B. Dr. B. was supposed to be the "Dr. Kolb" of New Jersey. I had made two previous appointments with him but didn't like his constant request for immediate and full payment of $2750. This time we were hoping a new set of eyes would help. The first hour of the appointment was a review of his background, achievements and work with the FDA. The next 45minutes consisted of a dry-eye test, booklets to read, a suggestion of a colonic and a better diet. This was a one-time visit that was less than desirable. He was no Dr. Kolb. On the way home, Stacy apologized to me for making us spend so much money and I replied that it would have been worth it if he had helped in any way shape or form, but he had not. Another major letdown!

On August 30th, Stacy, I and the kids went bowling and had lunch. It was a peaceful day. Stacy is seen in a picture throwing a kiss to me as I took their picture. September 1st was a small get together for her brother Randy's birthday. Only the immediate family was present. True to her legacy, Stacy played with the kids until she asked me to take her home. She was tired. She was hurting. The next evening, the immediate family went out for dinner for Randy's birthday. Alli, her sister-in-law remembers Stacy telling her that she would never miss her brother's birthday.

Stacy began having a problem vomiting, along with her diarrhea. She asked me to email Dr. L. to see if it were okay for her to take a medication called REGLAN. The Viberzi had stopped working. I sent a text to B., his assistant with the question and request. Seems Dr. L. was away on vacation until Tuesday. I picked up the prescription Tuesday afternoon. Stacy took the first pill around 1.

On Wednesday, September 4th, she stayed in bed all day. My sister dropped something off at the house and remarked that Stacy did not look well. Stacy complained that her gums and tongue felt funny. I responded that I would make a dental appointment. I left the house around 5, knowing Kevin and my husband were at a nearby park. No sooner did I arrive at home, I received a phone call on Facetime from my granddaughter, saying "mommy was in trouble, and she couldn't speak". I turned the car around and told her to stay on the phone and to show me Mommy. I visibly saw that her jaw was locked closed. I told her I had to use the phone and that I would be there shortly. I phoned my husband and told him there was an emergency and to get to the house immediately. When I arrived at the house, I saw Stacy laying on Barry, crying. EMS had arrived. She just had the reversed reaction, her jaw locked open, tongue flailing. The EMS said that they were only able to take her to the local hospital. I said, "never again". Got into the car and drove to our local trauma center.

On the way to the hospital Stacy's jaw locked shut again. She was concerned that she would chip her teeth. I made a mental note surprised that through all this, she was still concerned about her teeth. Her jaw was clenched shut very tightly. It hurt and she was frightened. When she was able to speak, she said to me, "Can't wait to see what they'll do to me again at our local trauma center". I said, "Hopefully it will be a good experience".

Arriving at the hospital, I parked in front of the ER and went to the desk, explaining that I thought she was having a stroke. At this time, Stacy threw up. She was taken to the back immediately, and I parked my car. She was given an EKG and placed on a gurney in the hallway. She was not seen by a physician for over an hour. When the doctor arrived, he said he was sure it was the Reglan that had caused this condition and that he had seen it before. I was actually "happy" that finally something seen, was known. He ordered one Benadryl pill. In less than an hour, Stacy had an "open mouthed" attack where her jaw was locked open, tongue moving from side to side. I had never seen anything like that and screamed for the nurse. I told her to get the doctor before it went away. The doctor. arrived and ordered intravenous Benadryl, which calmed down the jaw. A little over an hour later Stacy had another closed mouth attack. An hour after that she was discharged. Stacy was discharged with a prescription for Benadryl (1) tablet. The pharmacy would not fill it, saying we could buy it over the counter. On the way home I mentioned that finally we had a good experience. knowing the outcome now, I wonder, if (1) Benadryl could not do the trick the first time, why a prescription for (1) was written when sending her home. I feel that if Stacy had stayed overnight for observation, she may be alive today. Or maybe a stronger Benadryl could have loosened the jaw at home.

I stayed with Stacy the entire day Thursday. She was very groggy. I left for home when Kevin returned that night and went to the mall to buy her new shoes, as the next day was the "rehearsal dinner". My son Jeffrey was getting married on Saturday. I picked out 3 pairs and Face-Timed Stacy. She picked the one she liked best. Her dress was hanging on her dresser, ready to go.

The next morning, I was awakened by my cell phone. I always kept it on and right next to my bed in case of an emergency. I heard Kevin on the line. His voice made me jump up immediately. He said, "I don't think your daughter is with us anymore". I started screaming and ran directly towards the door. I threw my phone on the bed so Barry could talk to Kevin. I kept screaming all the way to Stacy's house. Please GOD let this be a mistake. Please GOD don't take my baby girl. NO NO NO, over and over. Arriving at the house I saw an ambulance and a police car there but mostly all I could focus on was Cameron and Sierra standing outside with Kevin. I hugged them both and ran up the stairs. The policeman would not let me into her room. I said I'm trained in CPR, he said he was also, but she was gone. I sat on the floor against the wall by her bathroom and cried and cried.

Dr. L. paid a shiva call to our house after Stacy passed. When I asked him why he wrote that script, he replied: "I got agitated when I saw the script for the additional milligram of valium, and I did not look at the other scripts, I just signed them. Had I known what it was for, I never would have prescribed it" To make matters worse, the pharmacist did not even catch the "severe drug interaction warning" with Stacys current medications either. Maybe the pharmacist should have not filled the script. I do not know..

She was buried in that blue sequined dress she had chosen for her brother's wedding.

STACY'S EULOGY

Ivy Davidoff

I lost my childhood best friend today - the first person to ever truly call your BEST. Stacy Shain, you left unexpectedly today.

You were the funniest most eccentric human and no one in the world knew anyone as secretly talented as you. You were my soul sister and swooped me up in 7th grade like a gift from the gods when I needed you the most. My entire childhood into adulthood you had a way of creating a bubble we lived in, while the world lived in another. It was a magical place to live and I loved living in recluse (your favorite word) with you. I couldn't even make a new friend or date without having them meet you, because until they did they simply wouldn't understand me as a person.

For someone in high school to not genuinely give a crap what anyone thinks and live the way you do is unheard of. You went through life beating to your own drum and I happily followed along because it was the safest and most fun place to be in the world. The fun was always where you were. The world was drinking at backyard pool parties late at night and you would be recording a video in my basement about the hidden world of Bin Laden and his multiple wives. Your talent was unmatched. You had the voice of an angel and could sing "Wind Beneath My Wings" better than Bette herself and could do stand-up in 3 seconds on any topic we gave you. I have seen you time and time again rip crab legs with your teeth and destroy all you can eat buffets all while remaining 100 lbs. You threatened the pilot of my flight en route to California leaving you one summer that if the flight had any issues, you'd tear the plane doors open with your teeth and save me. You were immortal from day 1.

I could tell you anything in the world. You saw the ugliest parts of me and were my biggest fan. You would make me laugh in times of crisis. There are people in this world that will never ever have a friend as funny as you – ever. You are such a part of me – our weird words, our hidden languages, terms that make no sense (calling someone a fluke or dip really isn't normal Stace…) We made complete sense together. We'd go on trips and my suitcase was packed days before and in perfect order. You'd swing by 5 minutes before with a broken suitcase, maybe some underwear and zero plans. This was the magic of you. You kept me down to earth and levelheaded when I took life too seriously.

You taught me how to love family above all else. Your love for your mother was unlike anything I've ever seen. Literally Bonnie + Clyde. You loved both of your brothers unconditionally and taught me to do the same on levels I didn't know were possible and brought me closer to my own. You three are as thick as thieves and you gave your children the best gift – each other. Your love for family shaped me as a wife and a mother.

You may no longer be here but for as long as I am on this earth your soul will live within mine. Love you pearl, I'll see you every time I eat lobster or ever attempt to sing.

ivy hillman

To the sister I never had:
from Allison

Gabriella gave this to me, and she wanted me to read it today since she could not come

Seeing aunt Stacy meant fun!

It meant playing hide-and-go-seek, going into Nani and Pa's attic, spinning around on the round outdoor table under the umbrella, sitting on a blanket and being pulled around the yard on the grass. If there were a party or a barbeque and Stacy was there, she'd have all the kids in a circle playing games. She was so much fun, but there was so much more to her. She couldn't bear to see anyone sad or in pain. Recently, my sister Alexa was very upset about something and Aunt Stacy kept her on the phone for an hour till she made her forget about her sadness.

Alexa wanted me to let aunt Stacy know that she promises she will never forget her and that she loves her so much.

I will never forget you. I can't-I have so many memories, so many sayings, so many moments, holidays, snow days. Your memories are everywhere for me and I'm so grateful for that. My daughters were the daughters you always dreamed of having until your very own "mini-me" was born. I will love Sierra and I will help her grow up without you. I will make sure she always knows the immense love you had for her. My daughters will always protect her like the little sister she is to them. I adore Cam and Jax and we will love them and make you proud in helping them as well.

You were so tortured these last few years. We lost so many memories. I am so grateful for our Disney trip and last Monday giving you one last hug and your typical "Stacy" text after each of our visits.

I find comfort knowing you are at peace now. I just wish we still had you here with us.

To my beautiful sister Stacy:
From your Brother Randy

To Know you was like knowing a true angel on Earth. You were true ray of light bringing joy to everyone who was lucky enough to be graced by your presence.

We were as tight as a brother and sister could be. You looked up to me. You protected me even though I was the one who was supposed to be protecting you. You loved me unconditionally and knew that I loved you back just the same.

I remember your jokes. Funniest person I ever knew. Your quick wit had everyone in tears. Your rap battles when we used to party-you could have battled Eminem and won-Funniest thing ever.

I remember your singing voice. The voice of an angel. Going far in many singing competitions. I always wondered how a girl so small could have such a powerful touching voice. I could listen to you sing all the time. I loved that about you.

You were the one who told me when I was wrong and explained how to make things right. You were my voice of reason. Even though you loved me so much, you loved me enough to give it to me straight. Thank you for knocking sense into me.

When you got sick, you tried to push us away, because you didn't want anyone to remember you that way. You wanted us to remember the old Stacy. The fun-loving Stacy, life of the party, lighting up the room. I wouldn't let you push me away. I forced myself back into your life, and anytime we were together it was like you were never sick. Ill cherish those times we had together for the rest of my life. I had NO idea it would be the last times I would see you. What I would give to hear your voice one more time. I would ask you to sing to me. To comfort me like you always did.

You were the most amazing mother. Even through your sickness, you fought the pain to play with them, and make videos to document those good times for them to remember. Don't worry, they will never forget. None of us will.

When I posted on Facebook about your passing, the outpouring support from family and YOUR friends was unbelievable. I loved reading everyone's stories about you. It brought me back to when times were good.

I am going to miss you more than you will ever know. But I know you will be watching over us, especially your beautiful kids.

I would like to end this with a poem from Elizabeth Frye, which gives me some comfort to know you will always be with us.

> *Do not stand at my grave and weep.*
> *I am not there; 'I do not sleep.*
> *I am a thousand winds that blow,*
> *I am the diamond glints on snow.*
> *I am the sun on ripened grain,*

I am the gentle autumn rain.
When you awaken in the morning's hush
I am the swift uplifting rush
Of quiet birds in circled flight,
I am the stars that shine at night.

On September 6, 2019 Stacy's funeral gathered more than 400 people.

Black lines forming on palms

Bumps that began to eminate from body

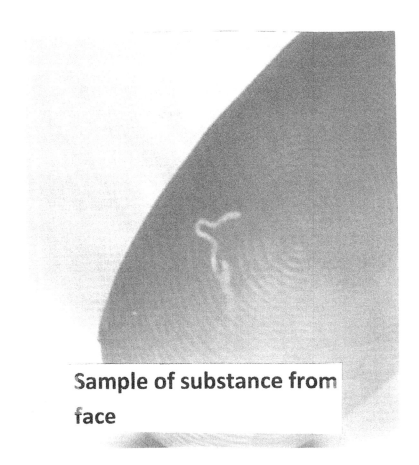

Sample of substance from face

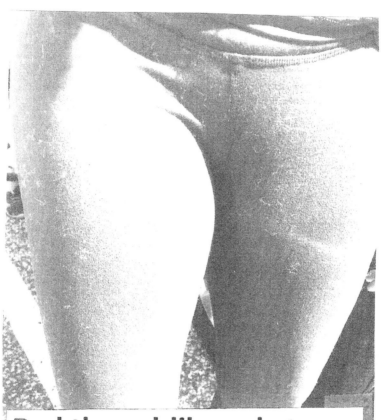

Red thread-like substance emerging from clothing

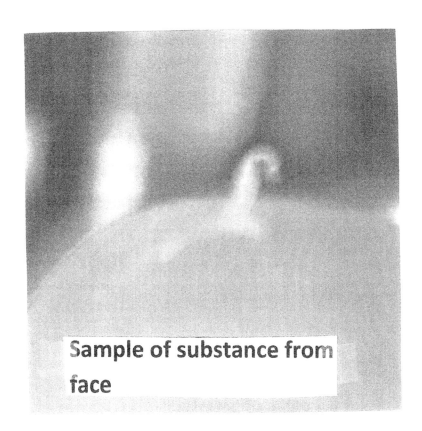

Sample of substance from face

Robert Wood Johnson | RWJBarnabas
University Hospital | HEALTH

One Robert Wood Johnson Place
P.O. Box 2601
New Brunswick, NJ 08903-2601

Phone: 732-828-3000

www.rwjuh.edu

January 18, 2019

Ms. Stacy Shain
24 Whirlaway Rd.
Manalapan, NJ 07726

Dear Ms. Shain,

I hope this letter finds you well. Thank you for taking the time to share your experience with us, regarding your visit to the Robert Wood Johnson University Hospital (RWJUH), 2West- OB Unit on January 14, 2019. We were made aware that you had the opportunity to speak with Navin Patibandla, Patient Representative on January 14, 2019 and had expressed concerns regarding the care you received on our 2West- OB unit.

We are continuously striving to improve the quality and service of care we provide and your feedback is very useful in helping us achieve the best results for all of our patients and families. Please know we take all concerns seriously and as a leadership and healthcare team, we have worked collaboratively in order to review your concerns.

Please be assured that the concerns you shared have been thoroughly reviewed by Hospital Leadership. In an effort to follow up with the concerns you shared with us, I was made aware that Ms. Keeba Souto, Nursing Director, 2West- OB, was able to connect with you on January 14, 2019, in-person, to discuss your concerns. Keeba shared that she reviewed your concerns and provided you with satisfactory follow-up. She also shared that she will use your feedback for improvement efforts.

We deeply value our relationship with you and all our patients and families who we partner with to meet their healthcare needs. In the meantime if there is anything else we may assist you with, please feel free to contact Ms. Keeba Souto at (732) 828-3000, Extension 3872 or any member of the Patient Experience Department at your convenience. The Patient Experience Department can be reached at the office between the hours of 8:30 a.m.-7:30p.m., Monday through Friday at (732) 828-3000, extension 8501.

If you would like a copy of your medical records, a request may be submitted in person to the Health Information Management department between the hours of 8:00am to 4:30pm, Monday through Friday. All requests for copies must be made in writing and must be signed by you, the patient. If the medical records are not for continued medical care, please be aware there are fees for processing.

Ms. Stacy Shain
January 18, 2019
Page 2

Robert Wood Johnson University Hospital's goal is to always provide quality, patient-centered care. We are grateful to you for conveying your concerns and we have utilized these comments to further improve our services in these areas.

Please accept our best wishes for continued health and well-being and thank you for choosing Robert Wood Johnson University Hospital for your healthcare needs.

Sincerely,

Leonard Bogatch
Patient Experience
Robert Wood Johnson University Hospital

Allergan Implant Complaint

1 message

Seland, Virginia <Virginia.Seland@fda.hhs.gov>   Thu, Apr 30, 2020 at 11:21 AM

To: Bonnie Shain <bonnieshain@gmail.com>

Good morning, Ms. Shain,

Thank you for your email. I am so very sorry to hear of your daughter Stacy's passing. Please accept my sincere condolences.

The complaint you filed with this agency on 8/02/2016 has been entered into the US Food and Drug Administration's (FDA) National Consumer Complaints database. It has been assigned consumer complaint # 146509. Your complaint has been forwarded to the proper personnel for review.

If you would like to receive the results of any follow-up to this complaint, you will need to file a Freedom of Information Act (FOIA) request. Instructions on how to file a FOIA can be found using the following link:
http://www.fda.gov/RegulatoryInformation/FOI/HowtoMakeaFOIARequest/default.htm.

Information is not released until the complaint has been closed and all follow-up completed. Please be sure to include your complaint number on all correspondence.

Thank you for contacting the US Food and Drug Administration with this important information.

Sincerely,

Ginny

COMPLAINT INFORMATION FORM COMPLAINT NUMBER:

		1. DATE OF COMPLAINT *(Month/Day/Year)* **July29,2016**
2. COMPLAINT RECEIVED	BY PHONE ☐ BY LETTER: ☐ BY FAX: ☐ BY E-MAIL: ☐ By Phone and email	**3. SOURCE OF COMPLAINT** x☐ CONSUMER ☐ OTHER:

4. **COMPLAINANT IDENTIFICATION**	a. NAME AND ADDRESS *(Include Zip Code)* **Stacy Shain** **24 whirlaway road** **manalapan nj 07726**	b. TEL. NUMBER: HOME 732-298-4772: WORK: CELL: 732-598-7206 c. FAX: d. E-MAIL:

5.COMPLAINTOR INJURY	a. DESCRIPTION OF COMPLAINT/INJURY My body is being oisoned by my Allergan silicone implants that were defective when they leaked into my body-My original complain were pins and needles in my arms and legs. pain in my chest and arms. I behan getting bumps in my throat, lung, face neck shoulders and chest. I severe head pain, brain and brain fog. I cannot sleep and was down to 95lbs at one point. My han shake and the bumps in my throat make it had to breathe and swallow. I have been to two ENT Physicians who dont know what to make of the spots. Ive been to an oncologist for the spot on my Ive been in touch with Sloan Kettering who says to monitor its growth. Ive been to dermatologists shrug their shoulders at the amount of tiny bumps all over my skin which is filled withsolution of some sort. My mother took me to Atlanta to Dr. Kolb who explantd the implanys and is now detoxi my body-She found both implants to be defective, she found grade 3 contractures on both sides s removed 6 infected lymph nodes-she found the implants to be leaking AND silicone immune dysfunction. I am still being treated with Dr. Kolb but am now a patient of Lifestyles Medical in W Long Branch NJ. I undergo Chelation as well as IV medication. I have tested myhair for chemic and was surprised at how many chemicals are in my body-I am awaiting the resumts of a urine chemical chemical testas well as a test for silicone-those tsts ar rare along with the amount of medical professionals who are not trained insilicone toxicity. Our FDA must listen and look at the amount of complaining and sick women and take this product off the market AGAIN.	b. DOES COMPLAINANT EXPECT ADDITIONAL FDA CONTACT? (1) ☐NO (2) x☐ YES *Remarks:* awaiting more tests and more medical problems C. PERMISSION TO GIVE INFORMATION TO STATE/OTHER GOVERNMENT AGENCY: (1) ☐NO (2) x☐ YES *Remark:* d. DID COMPLAINANT CONTACT THE MANUFACTURER: (1) ☐NO (2) ☐x YES *Remarks:* but have not made a complaint yet

7. **INJURY OR ILLNESS RESULTED** a. (1) ☐ NO (2) ☐XYES *(If "yes" complete items a through d)*	b. TYPE SYMPTOM 1. ☐VOMITING 2. ☐X NAUSEA 3. ☐XDIARRHEA 4. ☐XFEVER 5. ☐ XSKIN/EYE IRR. 6. X☐ HEADACHE 7. X OTHER	ONSET TIME(HRS) ⸱SINCE jAN 2016	DURATION HRS OR DAYS c. ATTENDING HEALTH PROFESSIONAL (1) ☐ NO (2) X☐ YES *(If "yes" give name, address, and phone number)* **dR. KOLB** **4370 georgetown square** **atlanta georgia-30338**
			d. ER☐ OR HOSPITALIZATION☐ (1) ☐ NO (2) ☐ YES *(If "yes" give name, address, phone number and dates)*Many hospital visits but mostly centra state medical center w main st. freehold nj 07728

8. **PRODUCT AND LABELING**	a. BRAND NAME **Allergan breast implant**	b. PRODUCT NAME
	c. SIZE AND PACKAGE TYPE **304.1cc**	d. NAME AND LOCATION.TEL # OF STORE WHERE PURCHASED **NYU School of Medicine**
	e. PACKAGE CODE/SERIAL NUMBER: SERIAL #: 14508125 UPC CODE:	
	DATE USE: **08-18-2010**	DID COMPLAINANT CONTACT STORE: (1) ☐NO (2) x☐ YES

MAYO
CLINIC   200 First Street SW
            Rochester, Minnesota 55905

'1 80   3 01   6 7 80

Ms. Stacy A. Shain
1102 Creamery Court
Freehold, NJ 07728-8542

June 23, 2017
RE: Ms. Stacy A. Shain
MC#: 10-711-805

Dear Ms. Shain:

Thank you for your request for an appointment in the Department of Neurology. We appreciate the confidence you have expressed in Mayo Clinic by requesting this appointment. Unfortunately, we are unable to offer you an appointment at this time.

Demand for appointments far exceeds our capacity to accommodate all requests. Therefore, appointment requests are prioritized based on the likelihood that we can provide additional tests or treatment options which will be beneficial or which are significantly different from evaluation or treatment already received. Your medical information was reviewed by our physician triage team and we are sorry to inform you we cannot offer you an appointment at this time.

If you feel there is additional critical information that may result in a more favorable decision, we would be happy to review the information. Please work with your other neurology providers to send us that information. Alternatively, one of your other providers may also contact our on-call physician who is available during regular business hours (8AM-5PM CST) Monday through Friday, at 507-284-1588.

Thank you for your consideration of Mayo Clinic for your neurological medical care needs. If your health situation changes we would appreciate another opportunity to evaluate whether our services can complement those provided by your current provider.

Sincerely,

Department of Neurology Appointment Office

kkn

State of New Jersey
DEPARTMENT OF BANKING AND INSURANCE
OFFICE OF THE COMMISSIONER
PO Box 325
TRENTON, NJ 08625-0325

TEL (609) 292-7272

CHRIS CHRISTIE
Governor

KIM GUADAGNO
Lt. Governor

RICHARD J. BADOLATO
Commissioner

October 13, 2017

Mr. and Mrs. Barry and Bonnie Shain
24 Whirlaway Road
Manalapan, NJ 07726

Dear Mr. and Mrs. Shain:

On behalf of Governor Chris Christie, I would like to thank you for your letter regarding the difficulties you have encountered obtaining reimbursement from a health care plan for medical services provided to your daughter. The Governor's Office has asked the New Jersey Department of Banking and Insurance to respond to your inquiry.

In order for the Department to address your situation we will require additional information about the insurance coverage involved including the full name of the plan and the policy ID number. We also require a brief description of your specific insurance difficulty and your permission for the Department to act on your behalf.

This information may be provided by completing and returning the enclosed assistance request form, or through our secure on-line assistance request form available in the "Consumers" section of the Department's web site at: http://www.state.nj.us/dobi/consumer.htm. Once the necessary information regarding the coverage involved has been received the Department will be in a position to contact the company.

Very truly yours,

Matthew Moench
Director of Legislation

Enclosure

L34382/vjo

LAB U160725-2187-1
PATIENT: Stacy A. Shain
ID: SHAIN-S-00003
SEX: Female
AGE: 31

(NT #: 40914
DOCTOR: Vincent Desanto, DO
Lifestyles Medical
107 Monmouth Rd 104d
West Long Branch, NJ 07764 U.S.A.

Toxic Metals; Urine

TOXIC METALS		RESULT µg/g creat	REFERENCE INTERVAL	WITHIN REFERENCE	OUTSIDE REFERENCE
Aluminum	(Al)	62	< 35		
Antimony	(Sb)	0.1	< 0.2		
Arsenic	(As)	8.7	< 80		
Barium	(Ba)	6.8	< 7		
Beryllium	(Be)	< dl	< 1		
Bismuth	(Bi)	< dl	< 4		
Cadmium	(Cd)	3	< 1		
Cesium	(Cs)	3.1	< 10		
Gadolinium	(Gd)	140	< 0.8		
Lead	(Pb)	4.7	< 2		
Mercury	(Hg)	< dl	< 4		
Nickel	(Ni)	22	< 10		
Palladium	(Pd)	< dl	< 0.15		
Platinum	(Pt)	< dl	< 0.1		
Tellurium	(Te)	< dl	< 0.5		
Thallium	(Tl)	0.4	< 0.5		
Thorium	(Th)	< dl	< 0.03		
Tin	(Sn)	0.2	< 5		
Tungsten	(W)	0.07	< 0.4		
Uranium	(U)	0.1	< 0.04		

URINE CREATININE	RESULT mg/dL	REFERENCE INTERVAL	-2SD	-1SD	MEAN	+1SD	+2SD
Creatinine	92.0	30- 225					

SPECIMEN DATA

Comments:

Date Collected: 07/21/2016
Date Received: 07/25/2016
Date Completed: 07/26/2016
Method: ICP-MS

pH upon receipt: Acceptable
<dl: less than detection limit
Provoking Agent:
Creatinine by Jaffe Method

Collection Period: timed: 6 hours
Volume:
Provocation:

Results are creatinine corrected to account for urine dilution variations. **Reference intervals and corresponding graphs
are representative of a healthy population under non-provoked conditions.** Chelation (provocation) agents can
increase urinary excretion of metals/elements.   V13

©DOCTOR'S DATA, INC. • ADDRESS: 3755 Illinois Avenue, St. Charles, IL 60174-2420 • CLIA ID NO: 14D0646470 • LAB DIR: Erlo Roth, MD
0001523

Date: 12/6/2016

Ms. Stacy Shain
24 Whirlway Rd.
Manalapan, NJ
07726

Innoval File No: 105762

By Mail

Dear Ms. Shain:

Your breast implants and capsular tissue, explanted by Dr. Kolb in Atlanta, Georgia on June 9, 2016, were received at my facility on July 27, 2016. I am sorry the wait has been so long before this material could be examined. We have been inundated with requests for our services, resulting in an extensive backlog. Thank you for your patience during this time.

The implants are identified as Allergan Style 15 smooth, round silicone gel-filled prostheses rated at 304 cc. Their fabrication attributes are nearly identical, supporting the opinion that they were made contemporaneously after 2010 but not made as a pair, as confirmed by different Lot Numbers.

The implants are not ruptured. Shell perforations are also absent. Both implants show fabrication defects which are visible to the eye unaided. On that basis, the implants should not have been deemed suitable for release into commerce, in particular the implant recovered from the right side. Neither implant would have been constrained within its capsule on the basis of the shell condition.

The capsular tissue was remarkable for severe adhesion to peripheral muscles. The condition is rarely encountered to that degree, least of all for implants with a brief in vivo dwell time. Intracapsular bleeding was demonstrated bilaterally through uptake of blood products by the capsules. The left capsule had distinct hematoma-like deposits confirming accumulation of blood at different times with consolidation into a discrete organized hematoma.

This is a Confirmation of Receipt/Briefing letter. IT IS NOT A REPORT. If you wish a report (Failure Analysis Report, as described in the attached briefing), please provide written or email directives (alphonsina@rogers.com). A $400.00 deposit is required with a report request (check or money order only payable to P. Blais). We still have a long list of clients awaiting reports as reports take a significant amount of time to prepare, especially if the client's implant history is complex. If a deposit is received, you will be added to the report list. On report completion, a Statement of Account would be issued and upon payment of the balance, the report would be mailed.

It is important to know a client's implant history. Medical records involving upper chest surgery are valuable (implantation, explantation, pathology reports) and can make the Innoval report more informative, in particular if the implant user has had more than one set of implants. In your situation, it is essential for me to have insight on your health. Observations on your capsular tissue establish significant variations from normal capsule formation. What is your health background? Are you under treatment now or have you ever been treated for a chronic disease? If records are unavailable, your best recollections as to exact surgery dates, the surgeon's name and the name of the facility/city where the surgeries took place would be helpful.

Yours truly,

P. Blais, Ph.D., F.C.I.C.

MTHFR Mutations

Methylenetetrahydrofolate reductase (MTHFR) is a gene that is responsible for producing an enzyme that converts folic acid to methylfolate, a bioavailable form of vitamin B9. Nutrient deficiencies of Vitamin B6, B12, and folate increase homocysteine levels which causes inflammation in the body. The ability of this gene to turn this switch on or off is crucial for the production of glutathione, the body's most important antioxidant.

Glutathione plays a major role in the body's detoxification of harmful, disease-causing toxins. When the body's ability to produce glutathione is decreased, secondary to genetic mutations like an MTHFR mutation, the disease process is enhanced due to the build-up of toxicity in the body. Disorders such as autism, ADHD, autoimmune diseases, multiple sclerosis, fibromyalgia, heart disease, addiction, and miscarriages have been linked to MTHFR mutations.

Glutathione's key role is the maintenance of intracellular redox balance (oxidation-reduction) and the detoxification of xenobiotics (a chemical or substance foreign to the body).

> *A defective MTHFR gene creates a vulnerability to disease processes as detoxification is impaired, leaving the body more susceptible to oxidative stress, and less tolerant of toxins such as heavy metals.*

When the function of the MTHFR gene is impacted by a genetic mutation, individuals may be at risk for a variety of health conditions, primarily due to the disruption of the methylation cycle. Methylation and demethylation act as on/off switches in the body that control all functions of the immune system, such as how the body fights infections and viruses, to regulation of the immune response.

Research has shown that impaired methylation is directly correlated with autoimmune conditions and is associated with neural tube defects, cerebrovascular and cardiovascular disease, inflammatory bowel disease, colorectal cancer, and psychiatric disorders.

HOW COMMON IS IT?

While the science is still out on the prevalence of MTHFR mutations, some say at least 40% of individuals and as high as 90% of children with ASD carry one mutation. Mutations come in various forms and some are more problematic than others. If one parent passes on a mutation of either the C677T or A1298C gene, an individual will have a heterozygous MTHFR mutation of either gene. If both parents pass on C677T or A1298C, the individual would have a homozygous mutation. In rare cases, a combination occurs whereby one parent passes on C677T and the other parent passes on A1298C. Both the homozygous and combination mutations have the greatest effect on a person's ability to produce glutathione. However, a single mutation of either gene also needs to be considered a risk factor and should be treated accordingly. Methylation can be decreased by 30% in those with a heterozygous mutation and up to 70% in those with homozygous MTHFR mutation.

MTHFR AND AUTISM

In children with ASD, the heterozygous allele frequency occurred in 56% of children in one study, whereby the frequency was significantly lower in the control group (41%). This could

This formation of clouds was spotted above Stacy's

brothers house, where her children often play and
sleep. It has drawn the attention of thousands who say
Stacy vcontinues to watch over all of us. White doves
have also appeared to remind us that Stacy's spirit is
still alive.

Made in the USA
Monee, IL
29 October 2020